King Sejong Invents an Alphabet

Carol Kim

illustrated by Cindy Kang

Albert Whitman & Company
Chicago, Illinois

Long ago in Korea, most children could not read and write.
Neither could their parents, or their grandparents, or their friends, or their neighbors.
All because Korea did not have an alphabet.

One king set out to change that.

When King Sejong was born in Gyeongbokgung Palace in 1397, his parents named him Yi Do. Because he was royalty, Yi Do learned to read and write Hanja, the complex Chinese characters Korea then used for an alphabet.

Yi Do had to spend many hours learning Hanja, but he didn't mind. He loved books more than anything. He would read them until he knew them by heart.

One day, young Yi Do discovered all of his books were missing. His father, King Taejong, worried that Yi Do spent too much time reading, so he'd ordered a servant to hide them. Yi Do tore apart his room. Where were his precious books?

There! Behind a screen—he found one overlooked book.
Joyfully, he read the book again and again. One hundred times...
then one hundred more.

Years later, when King Taejong was deciding who should succeed him as king, he realized his youngest son's love of learning and hard work would make him a great leader. In keeping with royal tradition, Yi Do's name was changed to Sejong, and he became king at the age of twenty-one.

As a ruler King Sejong forged his own path. Previous kings only paid attention to the elite yangban class. But Sejong believed his duty was to all of his subjects, especially the sangmin, or underprivileged, class.

"When the heavens nourish the earth," he wrote, "they do not distinguish between the great and the small. When a king loves his people, it should be the same."

One day, in 1432, a villager seriously harmed his own father on purpose.

King Sejong blamed himself. He believed he had failed to teach his people how to properly honor their parents. He ordered his staff to write a book filled with stories and pictures of children showing the utmost loyalty to their parents. In one story a son bravely defends his father after he is attacked by a tiger.

Copies of the book were handed out all over the country. But because the sangmin couldn't read, they could not fully understand the lessons.

Only the yangban had the time and money to learn the thousands of Chinese Hanja characters needed for reading. Hanja was a poor match for Korean sounds and words, so reading was difficult even for the yangban.

It was, King Sejong wrote, like "using a square handle for a round hole."

The solution came to him. Korea needed its own alphabet.
But could such a thing be done?

No one had ever invented an alphabet before. Other alphabets slowly developed over hundreds of years. Sejong's alphabet needed to be perfect. It needed to match the Korean spoken language and be simple to learn. It needed to be one that "a wise man can learn... in one morning...and a fool can learn...in the space of ten days."

Inventing an alphabet would also be risky, even for a king.
The yangban members of the government would be furious.
Knowledge was power, and the ruling class wanted the sangmin
to remain powerless.

If word of his plan got out, King Sejong knew that the yangban would try to stop him. He had to work in secret. Hardly anyone could be trusted enough to help him.

The king decided to base the shapes of the consonants on the shape of the mouth, tongue, and teeth when each sound was made. For example, the letter mi-eum (ㅁ) looks like the mouth when making an "em" sound. Ni-eun (ㄴ) looks like a raised tongue when making an "en" sound. Ki-yeok (ㄱ) looks like the tongue when making a "guh" sound.

Ten years of study went by. The king's health and eyesight began to fail. His doctors sent him to hot springs for medical treatment. But when he should have been resting, he pored over his books, studying, thinking, and writing.

Finally, in 1443, King Sejong released his alphabet of twenty-eight letters, which later came to be called Hangeul, or "the great script."

Immediately the protests began.

Ch'oe Mallie, a high-ranking scholar, believed the study of the Chinese language was important. He argued the alphabet was too simple. "I fear that the people will fall into laziness and never make efforts to learn."

Although most government leaders were against him, King Sejong published books using the new alphabet and rewrote public laws and notices so that everyone could understand them.

The yangban refused to use Hangeul.
But it opened up a new world for everyone else.

Now the sangmin could write protests to the government if they felt they had been treated unfairly. Farmers could read about new farming techniques and grow more crops.

Soldiers could write home to their wives and tell them how they wished they could see them.
Mothers could share their love through letters to their husbands and children.

And children could read books.
As many times as they wanted.

Eventually, Hangeul became the official Korean alphabet.
Today, both South and North Korea celebrate Hangeul Day
each year to honor King Sejong's greatest invention.

All because of a king who believed "The duty of a king is to love his people. That is all."

Why Hangeul Is Unique

What King Sejong set out to accomplish by creating a new alphabet was revolutionary. He clearly understood the stakes involved—abandoning a centuries-old practice of using Chinese characters meant bringing a powerful tool to the Korean underprivileged class.

Hangeul—known as Hunminjeongeum until 1912—is an unusual alphabet. Unlike other scripts, which evolved over long periods or were borrowed from other writing systems, Hangeul was created from scratch in a relatively short amount of time. Many people assume that spoken Korean is closely associated with the languages of China and Japan. But the truth is, Korean developed separately from these two languages and differs from them in important and fundamental ways.

An Ingenious Design

King Sejong designed the Korean alphabet with great care. He based the shapes of the consonants off of those made by a person's mouth, tongue, and teeth when they spoke each sound. The three main vowels represent the sky (·), the earth (—), and a person (|). The sky shape is not used on its own. It is combined with the other two vowels to create a total of ten. Unlike the English alphabet, each letter represents only one sound.

The letters are arranged into blocks for each syllable, and words are read from left to right.

The Korean Alphabet

Vowels ㅏ ㅑ ㅓ ㅕ ㅗ ㅛ ㅜ ㅠ ㅡ ㅣ
a ya ŏ yŏ o yo u yu ū i

Consonants ㄱ ㄴ ㄷ ㄹ ㅁ ㅂ ㅅ
k,g n t,d r,l m p,b s,sh

ㅇ ㅈ ㅊ ㅋ ㅌ ㅍ ㅎ
ch,j ch' k' t' p' h

Hangeul is amazingly easy to learn. In Korea today, most children know the alphabet before they are old enough to go to school. In contrast, before Hangeul, it took many years to learn the thousands of Chinese characters needed for basic reading.

The Great Debate

There are different theories about who actually created Hangeul. For a time, some scholars believed that Sejong assigned this task to members of the Hall of Worthies, a kind of intellectual think tank that he revived during his reign. Others gave the credit solely to Sejong, whose deep knowledge of languages made this theory believable. Indeed, Hangeul was officially announced with the declaration, "His Highness has personally created the twenty-eight letters of the Vernacular Script."

Today, the most widely held theory is that King Sejong was deeply involved in developing the letters, working closely with a small group pulled from the ranks of the Hall of Worthies. The reason no one knows for sure how Hangeul came to be created is because it is not mentioned in any official records. This is likely due to the need for secrecy while it was being developed.

A Long Journey to Acceptance

King Sejong lived only four more years after the release of Hangeul. Without him as a champion, the alphabet failed to be embraced by Koreans of influence and power. Over the next five hundred years, Hangeul was often ignored and sometimes banned outright.

But its ingenious simplicity helped keep the alphabet from disappearing completely. Marginalized people, such as women and monks, continued to use Hangeul. Preserving the alphabet was an act of national pride and identity for Koreans. This was especially significant during Japan's occupation of Korea from 1910 to 1945.

Finally, after Korea gained independence from Japan in 1946, Hangeul became the country's official alphabet, five centuries after its invention. It is widely used, and believed to be one of the main reasons most Koreans can read and write today.

King Sejong's legacy of Hangeul, along with many other remarkable improvements he made in the areas of agriculture, medicine, music, and astronomy earned him the title of "the Great" after his death. Today, because of King Sejong, almost every Korean knows how to read and write—one of the most important skills a person can have. He achieved his goal, as stated in his own words when he released the alphabet to the public: "It is my fervent hope that they improve the quality of life of all people."

Selected Sources

Diamond Sutra Recitation Group. *King Sejong the Great: The Everlasting Light of Korea*. New York: Diamond Sutra Recitation Group, 2010.

Kim-Cho, Sek Yen. *The Korean Alphabet of 1446: Expositions, OPA, the Visible Speech Sounds, Annotated Translation, Future Applicability*. Amherst, NY: Asea Culture Press; Humanity Books, 2002.

Kim-Renaud, Young-Key, editor. *The Korean Alphabet: Its History and Structure*. Honolulu, HI: University of Hawai'i Press, 1997.

King Seijong Memorial Society. *King Seijong the Great: A Biography of Korea's Most Famous King*. Seoul: King Seijong Memorial Society, 1970.

Koehler, Robert. *Hangeul: Korea's Unique Alphabet*. Seoul: Seoul Selection, 2010.

Source Notes

"When the heavens nourish the earth...": Diamond Sutra Recitation Group, editor. *King Sejong the Great: The Everlasting Light of Korea*, 23. New York: Diamond Sutra Recitation Group, 2010.

"using a square handle...": S.C.S., "How Was Hangul Invented?" *The Economist*, Oct. 2013.

"a wise man can learn...": S.C.S.

"I fear that the people...": Diamond Sutra Recitation Group, 90.

"The duty of a king...": Estudandohapkido, "Hangul - The Language of Compassion (English)." *YouTube*, Feb. 17, 2012.

"His Highness has personally created...": Diamond Sutra Recitation Group, 87.

"It is my fervent hope...": Lee, Ji-young. *Hangeul: The Understanding Korea Series*, 28. Seongnam-si: The Academy of Korean Studies Press, 2013.

For my mother and father, thank you for inspiring me—Carol Kim

To my family and closest friends—Cindy Kang

Library of Congress Cataloging-in-Publication data is on file with the publisher.

Text copyright © 2021 by Carol Kim
Illustrations copyright © 2021 by Albert Whitman & Company
Illustrations by Cindy Kang
First published in the United States of America in 2021 by Albert Whitman & Company
ISBN 978-0-8075-4161-6 (hardcover)
ISBN 978-0-8075-4162-3 (ebook)

Printed in China
10 9 8 7 6 5 4 3 2 WKT 26 25 24 23 22 21

Design by Valerie Hernández

For more information about Albert Whitman & Company,
visit our website at www.albertwhitman.com.